MW01601122

Savage Survivor

300 Million Years of the Shark

Dale Copps

Westwind Press

1 2 3 4 5 6 7 8 9 0   80 79 78 77 76

Library of Congress Number: 75-38744

Printed in the United States of America.

Published by Westwind Press, A Division of
             Raintree Publishers Limited
             Milwaukee, Wisconsin 53203

Distributed to the trade by
             Follett Publishing Company
             1010 West Washington Street
             Chicago, Illinois 60607

             Library Edition L-0663
             Trade Edition T-0663

Library of Congress Cataloging in Publication Data

Copps, Dale G
    Savage survivor: 300 million years of the shark.

    SUMMARY: Describes the evolution and biology of
sharks, the legends about them, and their relation-
ship with humans.
    1. Sharks — Juvenile literature. [1. Sharks.
2. Fishes] I. Title.
QL638.9.C63   597'.31   75-38744
ISBN 0-8172-0502-0
ISBN 0-8172-0503-9 lib. bdg.

for J. B.

I wish to thank Patricia Bird of the Mote Marine Laboratory in Sarasota, Florida, for her careful reading and scientific evaluation of the manuscript.

I thank especially Dr. H. David Baldridge, also of Mote Marine Laboratory, for his steadfast assistance with this book. Dr. Baldridge not only wrote the foreword, but guided the manuscript through several drafts, offering encouragement along with the most current scientific information available. His partnership in the finished work was invaluable and I am most grateful.

Foreword

How arrogant it is for man to sit in judgment of the shark! Because we do not understand him, we call him unpredictable. We test him in terms of our own capabilities and brand him unintelligent. He has not changed significantly in millions of years, so we say that he is primitive. Since his way of life is at times in violent conflict with that of humans, we call him a man-eater. Many fear him. Some hate him.

Yet the shark is truly a marvelously designed animal. Evolution has not altered sharks in any meaningful way since long before man made his appearance on earth. When a design is good, there is no need to put out a new model every year. And a shark certainly is well designed for the purpose of being a shark. He does not do the cute tricks of a dolphin, and it is not easy for him to master simple tasks assigned to him by scientists. Tricks and meaningless tasks are not important parts of a shark's way of life — certainly not matters of life and death. And life to a shark is simply a matter of death. He is without doubt the ultimate predator.

If we consider intelligence as a measure of the efficiency by which an animal gathers information from its environment and makes use of that information for its own survival, then sharks have few equals. Their eyesight is only as good as it has to be, for the need to see prey at long distances is one thing for the hawk or the eagle in the bright skies and quite another thing for the shark in the dimly lit depths of the sea. On the other hand, the shark's capacity for detecting and interpreting sounds and other disturbances in the water is not even approached by the sophisticated electronic gadgetry of human submarines and divers. We speak lightly and unknowingly about extrasensory perception and auras as possible future communication links with other humans, animals, and possibly even plants. Yet for perhaps millions of years, sharks have been able to detect very minute changes in their electrical surroundings — unintended signals that can very quickly betray the hiding place of prey. The shark's uncanny ability to sense odors is legendary. And scientists recognize the presence of still other sense organs in the bodies of sharks, but know nothing of the use to which the sharks might put them. Can we call sharks primitive animals? Primitive in terms of having what it takes to be extremely efficient predators in the demanding environment of the sea?

Is the shark really unpredictable, or is it simply that our growing knowledge of him is still so limited that we can forecast his behavior only in the most gross of terms? Scientists have learned more about sharks in the past two decades than in all earlier time, yet sharks are not becoming more predictable; it is simply that we scientists are slowly becoming less ignorant of their ways.

The word "SHARK!" usually brings to mind the sight of a gigantic demonic fish bearing down on some hapless human. Such is the case at times, but far less often and with far less ferocity than most of us have been led to believe. The shark is by design a predator, and man in the sea is clearly an interloper. Anyone who enters the sea should realize that his presence is very quickly detected and evaluated by all forms of marine life, including sharks. The choice to do something in response to our trespass of the sea rests with those animals It is not under our control. The fact that sharks, out of literally millions of opportunities, choose to respond violently only a few dozen times throughout the world each year should be somewhat comforting rather than terrifying.

In bringing his understanding of sharks to you, Dale Copps clearly has become one of "us" — those people in whom fear of sharks has been replaced by respect bordering on admiration. Mr. Copps touches on many of the reasons why sharks have survived on this planet for so many millions of years. You will see that sharks have evolved so as to complement and fit better into their environment, thereby insuring their survival. Man, on the other hand, has chosen to drastically change his environment to meet his momentary demands. The effects of man's impatience are becoming increasingly apparent after only the first few thousands of years of his presence on this planet. With this perspective in mind, consider what Dale Copps has to say. Then decide for yourself: Of the two species, man and sharks, which is the intelligent one and which is the dumb one?

H. David Baldridge, Ph.D.
Senior Research Associate
Mote Marine Laboratory
Captain, U.S. Navy (Ret.)

Contents

Savage Survivor

1
Attack

He comes from the pelagic sea — the deep sea — moving north and inland, following the warm waters of midsummer. His huge form moves silently, almost weightlessly, through the cool blue waters off the New Jersey coast. His tail, or caudal fin, sweeps like a fluid crescent moon through the sea, propelling him forward. Its force tends to drive him downward. To counteract this, his two great pectoral fins are thrust out at his sides. At times, his sleek head moves from side to side through the waters. All of his senses are attuned to the clear, fluid world through which he moves. Perhaps he can only see a few feet in front of him, but he can *smell* the sea for hundreds of yards around him. And he hears sounds a mile or more away.

He is eight and a half feet long, and weighs close to half a ton.

He is *Carcharodon carcharias* — the great white shark.

And he is feeding.

Charles VanZant is a young man who loves the ocean. He is a strong swimmer, and this day, off the coast of Beach Haven, New Jersey, he turns in the water and looks inland, a hundred yards to the shore. Weary from his strenuous swim, he treads water for a few moments, enjoying the clear, warm

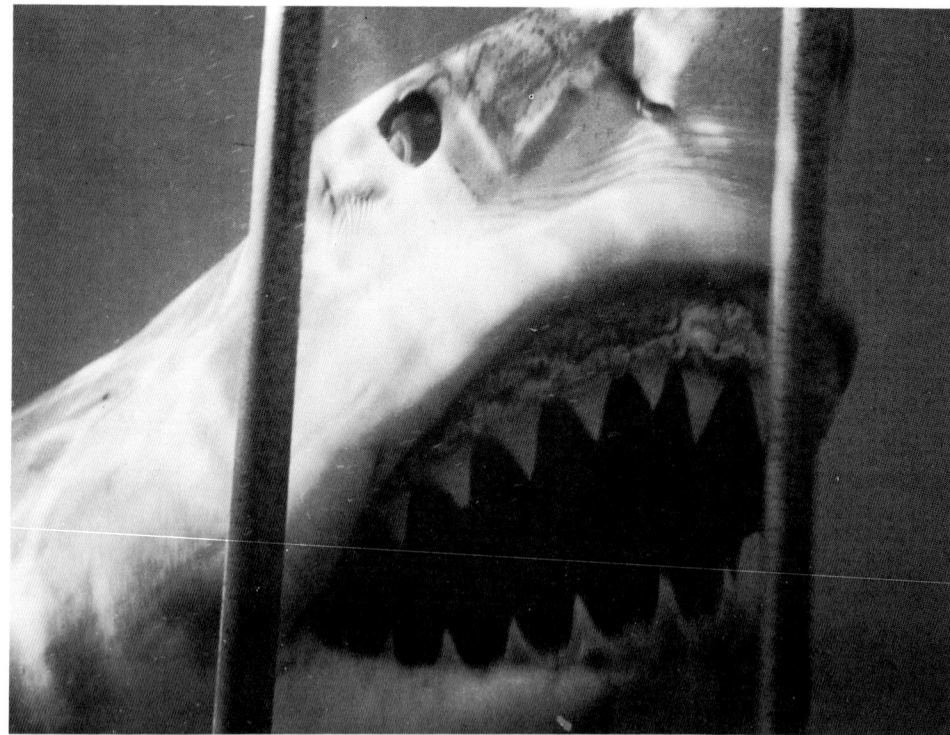
The great white shark.

day and listening to the crowds of happy bathers on the beach. Then, with a deep breath and renewed energy, he begins the swim back to the beach.

The shark senses his prey. From two football-field lengths away, he hears the vibrations set up by VanZant treading the water. Instinctively he turns and swims in a sudden burst of speed to within a hundred yards of the young man, where he begins to smell his prey. At once the ocean, and all the world, cease to exist for him. The feel of the water surrounding him, the tiny pilot fish that has accompanied him since morning — the million and one other sights, smells, and sounds of the great watery universe in which the shark lives — vanish from his notice. All that remains is the tiny but now overwhelming call of the target that lies on the surface of the water just ahead. Nothing short of a massive, fatal attack will turn him now from his necessary pursuit. Within a few yards he is in sight of his prey

— two moving white forms in the midst of the darker sea.

He attacks.

The searing sensation VanZant feels in his left leg causes him more fright than pain. He wonders what has happened. Suddenly, all around him the sea turns red, and he knows.

Driven to a frenzy by the smell of blood suddenly released to his senses, the shark attacks again, taking into his mouth both of the dangling white forms. Though his jaws can snap these great hunks of food in two, and he can swallow them whole, he does not. Why he does not is a question no scientist can answer for sure, but he does not.

Barely 50 yards from shore now, VanZant screams for help, then is pulled under the water by the furious thrashing of the monster that holds his legs. A hand from somewhere grabs VanZant's arm — help from shore—and he feels himself being pulled in two directions at once. The shark, now strangely quiet after his first two strikes, holds to the young man's legs as he is pulled toward the beach by the half dozen swimmers who have come to VanZant's rescue. Before they reach the shore, VanZant faints.

Suddenly, to the shark's senses, come many other smells and sounds, similar but not the same as those which first drew his attention. Yet he does not attack anyone else. Why he does not is another mystery to science. As the shark is dragged to the shallower waters near the shore, his senses pick up the falling depth of the water, the rising temperature closer to the beach. There, in barely two feet of water, he releases his grip, turns, and flees back to the deep sea — the pelagic sea — from which he has come.

The date was July 2, 1916. Charles VanZant died of shock and blood loss. His was the first fatality from shark attack recorded that far north in the United States in modern times. But far from the last.

Shark attack. The words seem to belong together. For as long as man has sailed the seas or dived beneath its waves for business or pleasure, he has known shark attack.

For centuries, in fact, that was practically *all* we knew about the shark. Even today, our knowledge of these creatures is far from complete. It's understandable that we should know more about cats and dogs, for instance, than we know about animals that roam the world and have an occasional, upsetting tendency to eat us.

Indeed, one of the themes of this book is man's ignorance. We have called the shark a god and a devil. We have cursed him for a scavenging, ocean-going vulture and credited him with destructive powers far beyond those of any living creature. We have placed him on a pedestal to worship, and we have torn him apart with our bare hands. But we have rarely understood him.

In recent years, thanks in large measure to the very ferocious habits that make us fear sharks so much, scientists have been studying them with greater concentration than ever before.

Shark research, however, is not without its problems. Real knowledge of a living thing can only be gained by observing it in its natural environment over a period of thousands of hours. Obviously this is impossible with a 2,000-pound great white shark constantly moving at a high rate of speed. Then, too, sharks are very expensive when bought for experimentation, and most types do not do well in captivity. But the more that is learned, the more fascinating and awesome the shark becomes.

This book covers much information on shark research. It does not pretend to cover the subject completely, but it does present the most current efforts being made to understand the mystery that is the shark.

2

A Marueilous Straunge Fishe

The beginning of wisdom is to call things by their right names.

Chinese proverb

The Name

He is *Haifisch* to the Germans, *tiburón* to the Spanish, and *requin* to the French. *Requin* means requiem, a hymn for the dead, and this perhaps reveals how French sailors felt about meeting the shark. It wasn't until the 16th century that the word "shark" came into common English usage. The source of this name is a mystery.

From the *Oxford English Dictionary:*

Shark (ʃɑɹk) . . . [Of obscure origin. The word seems to have been introduced by the sailors of Captain Hawkins's expedition, who brought home a specimen which was exhibited in London in 1569. The source from which they obtained the word has not been ascertained. . . .]
1. A selachian fish of the suborder Squali . . .; in the popular languages chiefly applied to the large voracious fishes of this suborder. . . .
1596 in *B.L. Ballads & Broadsides.* . . . There is no proper name for it [a 'marueilous straunge Fishe'] that I know, but that sertayne men of Captayne Haukinses doth call it a sharke. . . .

So 1596 is the first year we encounter the word "shark," but how the crew of "Captayne Haukinses" came upon the word, no one knows.

Older Than the Hills

Sharks are literally older than the hills. It is almost impossible to imagine how long they have been swimming the seas.

Between two and ten million years ago, the great mountain ranges of the Alps and the Himalayas were formed. Sharks were around then — and had been for a long time.

Two hundred million years ago, dinosaurs roamed the earth. But the seas already knew the shark — and the shark continued to thrive as the dinosaur fell to extinction.

Scientists believe that sharks were developing during the Devonian period, some 400 million years ago. They are probably as old or older than any form of life that has ever existed on land.

A five-foot nurse shark swims among a school of margate fish along a Caribbean reef.

But what is even more amazing is that the shark has come down through the last 300 million years virtually unchanged in structure. He is a living moment of prehistory. And in all likelihood he will survive into "posthistory" as well, after man has finally polluted or detonated or overpopulated himself off the face of the earth.

Just What is a Shark?

The word "shark" is used to describe about 300 different species of animal, roughly divided into 20 major families. When we speak of "species" and "families" we must be careful to note that the work of classifying the different sharks, even of naming some, is still going on. As scientists find similarities between two or more distinct types, or species, of sharks, they put them into families, like the terrier and spaniel families of dogs. But scientists do not yet agree on even the number of species there are, let alone how to properly divide them into families. As it becomes necessary to mention families when discussing similar species, the arrangement proposed by French scientist Paul Budker will be used.

Sharks range in size from the midwater shark (Squaliolus laticaudus), measuring only four to seven inches when fully grown, to the whale shark (Rhincodon typus), known to reach 50 feet and believed to grow even larger. The whale shark is a great, humpbacked beast, given to lolling around in very deep water. Occasionally one will surface and move about with a somber slowness, enjoying the sun. Whale sharks are so slow and unobservant that they are sometimes rammed and even killed by boats; this can be a real shock to crew and passengers, even on relatively large vessels.

The vast majority of sharks will not attack people, and pose no real threat to them. The whale shark, for example, feeds almost exclusively on plankton, which it filters from the sea water through a sieve-like structure. Its teeth are very small and possibly have no function at all.

The whale shark is the largest of all sharks, and is considered to be harmless. Whale sharks typically swim with their mouths open, straining microscopic plankton through a series of gill rakers in their throats.

Basically, sharks are fish, and share much with the 20,000 other species of fish that swim in their waters. But there are differences. Unlike most other fish, sharks don't have bones. Their skeletons are made up entirely of cartilege, a rough, elastic tissue, gristly and hard, but not as hard as bone. Our nose is supported by cartilege, for example, and we have it in other parts of our bodies as well.

Sharks are not the only fish that have cartilaginous skeletons. Rays and skates are two other examples. But rays and skates are flat, and their gill slits, used in breathing, are located on the underside of their bodies. Sharks have rounded bodies with gill slits at least partially on the sides.

Sharks differ from bony fish in a number of other ways. Bony fish have only one gill opening on each side of their heads. Sharks have between five and

8

seven separate openings on each side. Internal fertilization is the method of reproduction in sharks; in most bony fish, the male fertilizes the eggs after they have left the female's body. Most sharks can neither brake their forward motion nor swim in reverse, as bony fish can — they can only swerve to avoid collisions.

Bony fish have smooth, round scales over their bodies. Sharks are covered with denticles—sharp, teeth-like protrusions that can cause injury to anything or anybody brushing up against them.

Perhaps the most significant difference is that sharks, unlike most bony fish, have no swim bladders—organs that keep fish suspended in the water when they stop swimming. When sharks stop swimming, they sink. For many species, this can eventually mean death.

All fish breathe by passing water over their blood-laden gill surfaces and through their gill slits. Part of the dissolved oxygen is removed from the water,

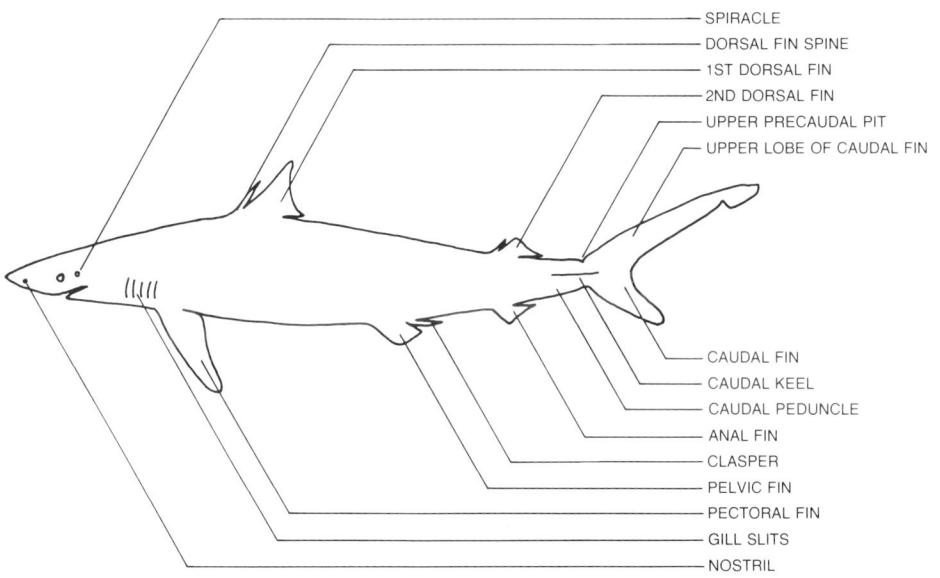

SPIRACLE
DORSAL FIN SPINE
1ST DORSAL FIN
2ND DORSAL FIN
UPPER PRECAUDAL PIT
UPPER LOBE OF CAUDAL FIN

CAUDAL FIN
CAUDAL KEEL
CAUDAL PEDUNCLE
ANAL FIN
CLASPER
PELVIC FIN
PECTORAL FIN
GILL SLITS
NOSTRIL

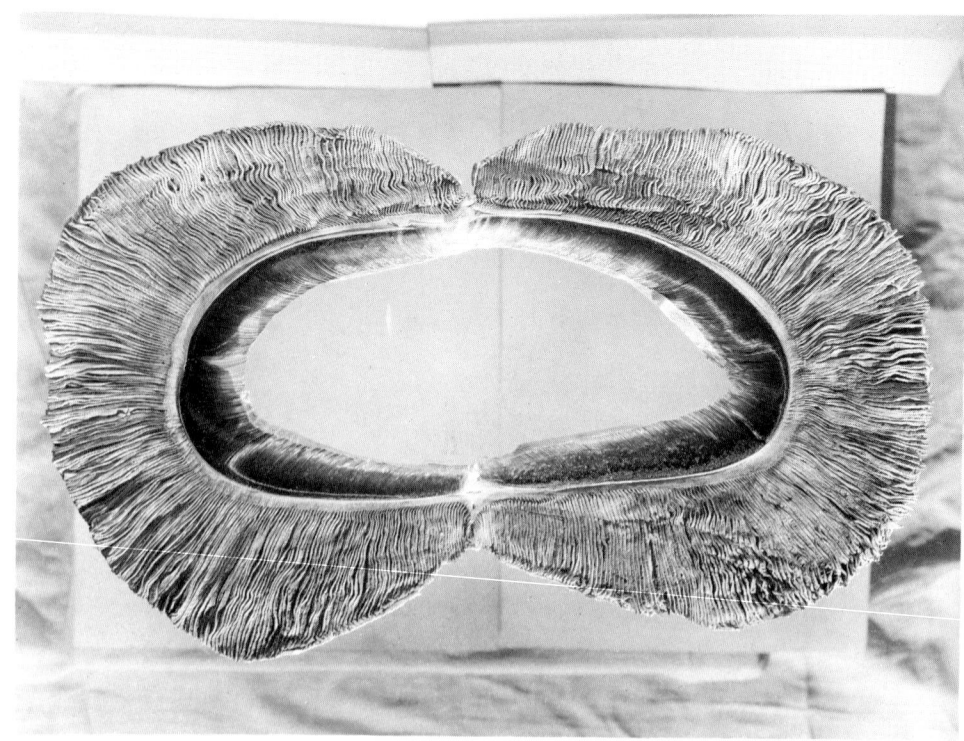

The dissected gills of a basking shark. They do double service in dissolving oxygen from the water and filtering plankton for food.

which then passes through the gill openings. To continue the flow of water, most species of shark must swim. Some have an opening in the head, called the spiracle, which pumps water to the gills when the shark is at rest. Others, however, must move almost continuously from birth to death, or they will suffocate.

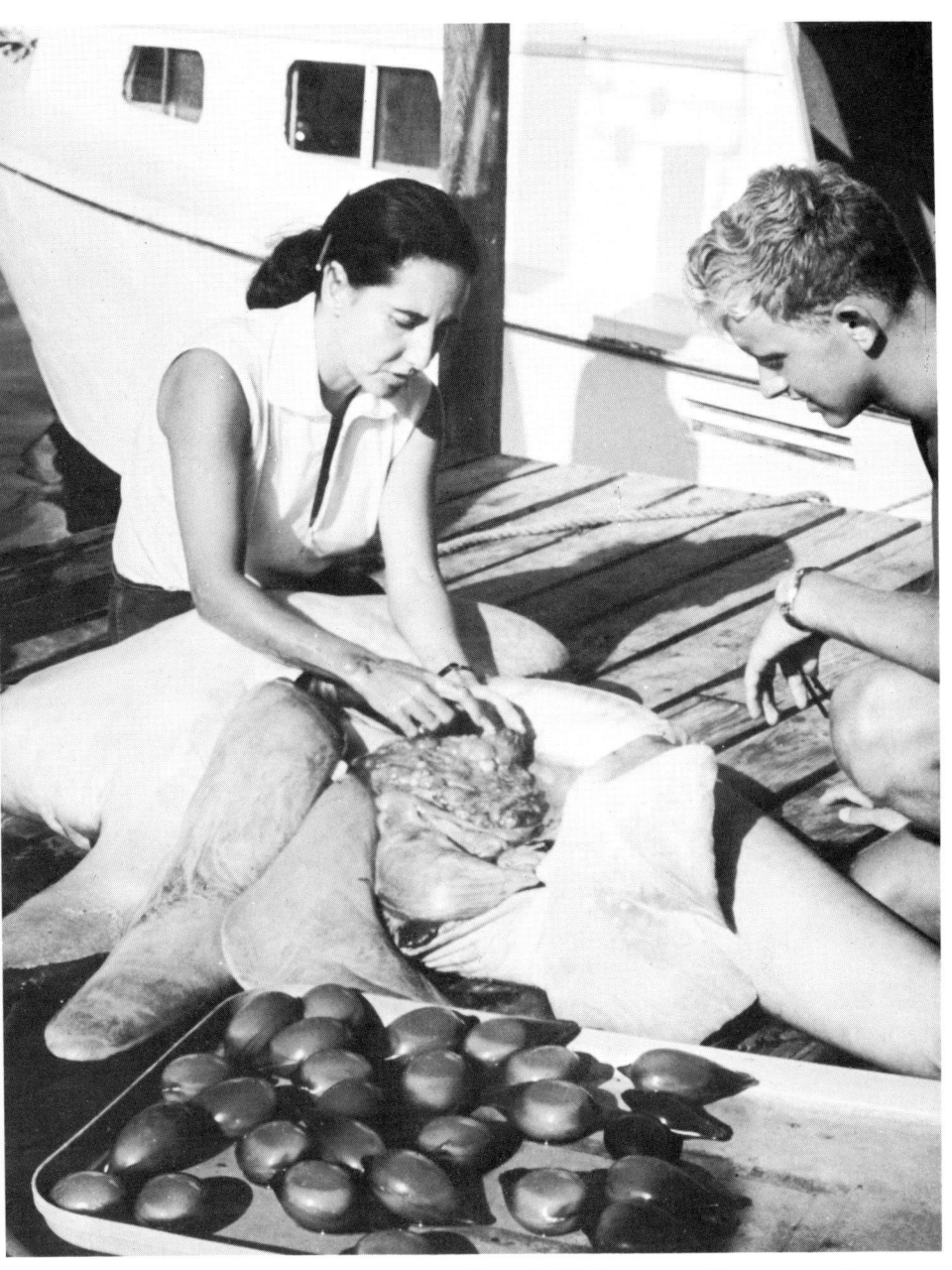

Shark expert Eugenie Clark removes the many embryo sacs from a pregnant nurse shark.

3
Feeding Machine

And they raved for food with increasing frenzy, being always anhungered and never abating the gluttony of their terrible maw: for what food shall be sufficient to fill the void of their belly or enough to satisfy and give respite to their insatiable jaws?

Oppian, Fishing, A.D. *100*

The Jaws

A prehistoric ancestor of the shark had jaws wide enough to accommodate a small car. Some great white sharks grow so huge they can swallow a pony. A person is no problem at all.

If there is one thing about the shark that terrifies mankind, it is his jaws — gaping wide and horrible, lined from front to back with razor-sharp teeth.

Shark scientist Dr. Perry W. Gilbert of the Mote Marine Laboratory in Florida has tested the strength of their bite. He found that some sharks can bite with the pressure of 18 metric tons per square inch — more than enough to snap a solid, quarter-inch steel cable under stress.

Actually, the shark's teeth are rather loosely implanted in the tooth bed; they are not even as firmly set as human teeth. Quite often, sharks lose teeth during an attack, as they are meant to. Behind the functional teeth are multiple rows (five or six or perhaps more) of spare teeth. These spares are al-

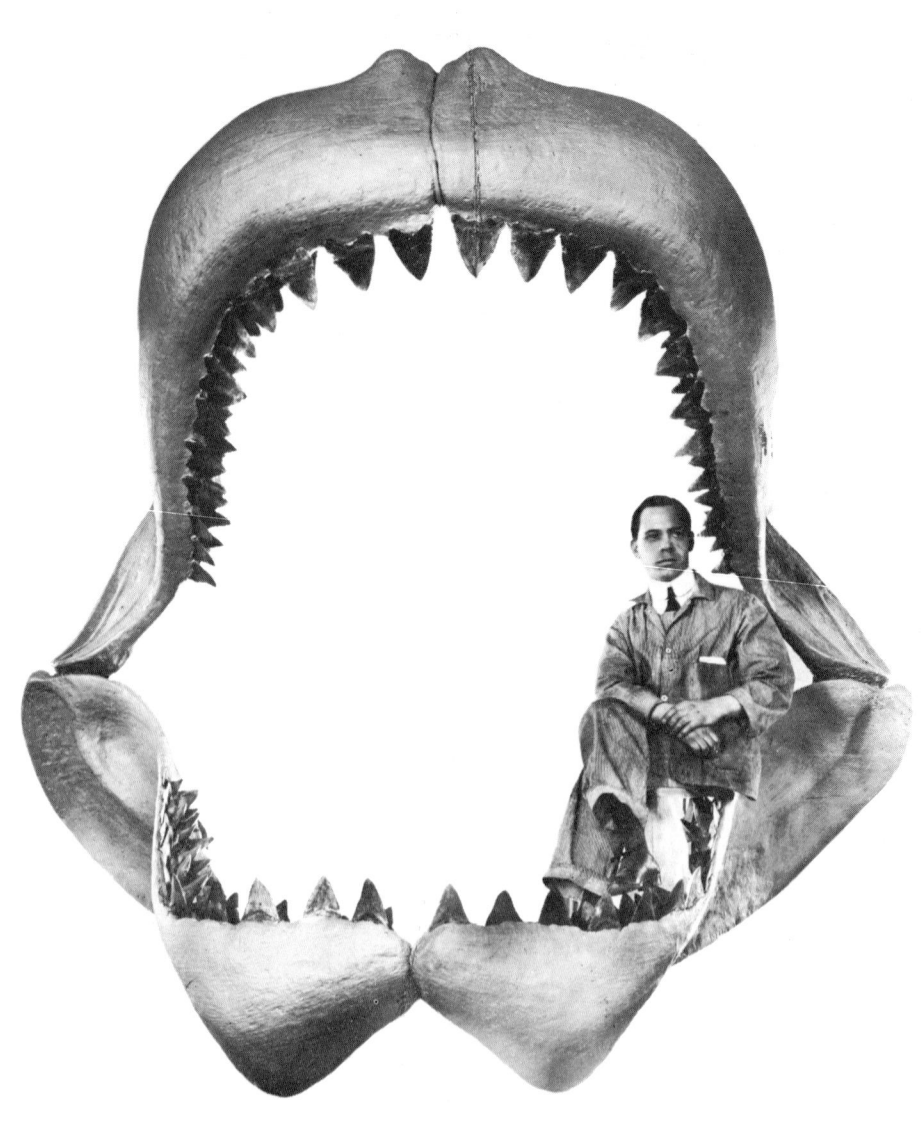

This monstrous *Carcharodon megalodon* jaw was reconstructed from the evidence of fossilized teeth, since the actual jaw cartilege had long deteriorated.

ways moving up slowly and replacing the functional teeth, rather like adult teeth in humans forcing out the baby teeth. If you pull back the protective covering in the jaws of a shark, you can see these rows of spare teeth, lying flat against the jaw. This mouthful of teeth was shared by meat-eating dinosaurs, extinct now for 70 million years.

Sharks who attack people often leave one or more of their teeth behind. Scientists use the teeth to identify the culprits. The white shark's teeth are very distinctive and often have been found in their victims. Scientists who have handled these teeth say they are sharp enough to shave arm hair.

In most sharks, the jaws are positioned well under the head, and for years it was believed they had to turn on their sides, or even upside-down, to get at their prey. Actually, such contortions are unnecessary. As the shark confronts his prey, his upper jaw

The rows of teeth in a tiger shark. The notched teeth distinguish this very vicious species.

moves forward from its quite loose anchoring in the head, the snout bends upward, and the victim is suddenly confronted with a cavernous mouth, bordered by many awesome teeth.

Once the prey is grasped, the shark tears a chunk from it and swallows it whole. This is easy for him. People have a long, relatively thin tube, called the esophagus, through which food passes on the way to the stomach. Sharks have hardly any esophagal region at all; the back of their mouth enters almost directly into the stomach.

In 1594, a man named Heinrich Herman Frey used this fact to speculate about Jonah and the "whale." In the Biblical story, Jonah is swallowed by what actually is described as a "great fish," only to be thrown up later, unharmed. To Frey, the story sounded more in keeping with the habits and abilities of a great white shark than those of a whale. Not only can these sharks swallow men whole; they also can evert their stomachs — almost turn them inside-out — in order to get rid of indigestible substances.

Furthermore, the shark's digestive system, still something of a mystery to scientists, apparently could have accommodated Jonah. Sharks can preserve food in their stomachs for unknown lengths of time before digesting it. How or why they are able to do this not known. But sharks appear to eat whenever they want to and digest whenever they must.

Dinner Bell

Sharks have been described as feeding machines. It was once believed they ate their weight in food every day. But the truth is that sharks feed irregularly. The basking shark (Cetorhinus maximus) is second only to the whale shark in size, and like the whale shark, feeds on plankton. During the summer months, the basking shark feeds continuously, swimming slowly along the surface, straining millions of pounds of sea water every hour. During the winter, however, when plankton is scarce, the basking shark sheds the gill rakers used in straining. He then sinks to the ocean floor and hibernates until spring.

But even when food is available year round, most species of shark feed irregularly and unpredictably. Sharks in captivity generally eat only 3 to 14 percent of their own weight in a week. In captivity or out, they may go for long periods without eating.

Until very recently, scientists believed that when sharks stopped feeding, they lived off fat stored in their massive, double-lobed livers. The liver may account for 25 percent of his total weight, and sharks with empty stomachs normally have reduced livers.

However, it is now believed liver weight shrinks with body weight, not in order to sustain the shark, but to maintain proper buoyancy in the water. In other words, the liver may do some of the work of the swim bladder in bony fish, alternately growing and shrinking to maintain the shark's careful weight balance in the water. Indeed, a shark weighing many hundreds of pounds out of the water may, because of this balancing mechanism, weigh only 10 to 15 pounds in the water.

Why sharks feed irregularly is still a mystery, though part of it has to do with their breeding cycle. During times of mating and giving birth, a necessary "feeding inhibition" is set up in sharks. The males, particularly in the larger species, tend to stop feeding before mating with the females.

Courtship and mating can be rough in large species. The male has to torment and hassle the female to get her cooperation. It is best in these times that the internal dinner bell be turned off. Sharks are known for their cannibalism.

If the female is actively uncooperative in mating, the male is in big trouble. Mature females, on the average, are 15 to 25 percent larger than the males — and just as cannibalistic.

A wide-eyed, newborn tiger shark, eager for adventure and dinner. The distinctive coloration on his back will fade and probably disappear as he gets older.

Females of many species move to shallow waters and give birth in special nursing areas. Newborn sharks generally are capable of caring for themselves from the moment of birth. And a good thing. The mother shark spends as little time as possible in the nursing area, and is inhibited from feeding while there. If her feeding inhibition weren't operating, she probably would eat her own children.

Baby sharks begin their lives as fully developed, miniature copies of their parents. To be sure, they are not sexually mature, but all the apparatus needed for swimming and hunting is ready for operation at birth.

Most species of shark give birth to live young. One exception is the whale shark. A single whale shark egg has been found for study — before it was found, whale shark reproduction was a mystery.

The egg case was a foot long, and inside was a 14½-inch embryo closely resembling the adult whale shark — right down to the distinctive spots on its back.

Shark litters are relatively small — two to perhaps 70 or 80 young. Bony fish need to lay tens of millions of eggs, since most are eaten or otherwise destroyed long before they hatch. Shark litters are much smaller because young sharks are better able to take care of themselves, and a greater number survive into adulthood.

Time to Eat

Scientists have not been able to prove that sharks have a sense of hunger. Some feel that, except in times of feeding inhibition, sharks are always impelled by a steady, low level of hunger.

Time and again, divers have reported contradictory tales about sharks. No one knows why one shark will attack and feed, while another will pass food by.

Once, while diving, ocean explorer Jacques-Yves Cousteau found himself almost face to face with a great white shark, the most ravenous of man-eaters. The shark seemed unaware of Cousteau until he was quite close. Then, all of a sudden, he noticed the diver and with a jerk of fright all but somersaulted in the water and fled. Though Cousteau was grateful, he cannot explain the shark's strange behavior. Nor can any other scientist.

But when the internal mechanism of the shark signals for food, however this happens, there is set in motion a predatory search and a violent destruction such as no other animal can demonstrate. And it all happens with such mechanical efficiency and singleminded devotion as to fill the strongest hearts with fear.

Sharks are singularly well-equipped to stalk their prey. Their sense of hearing, which has been tested in only a few species, is almost miraculous. Most of the sounds in the sea are of either too high or too low a frequency for humans to hear. The shark, however, can hear low frequency, pulsed sounds from as far away as 200 yards. He can hear other sounds from a good deal farther away — up to thousands of yards. His ears, unlike those of bony fish, are open to the sea. They are located behind the eyes.

More amazing still is the fact that sharks actually can *hear* with their *bodies.* They have a system of lateral line canals, filled with fluid, that extend from the head to the beginning of the tail on each side of the body. It is believed that these canals pick up sounds and movements in the water through a combined sensation of hearing and touch. Often the first signal of prey comes to the shark through his ears and through these canals.

Another unique feature of sharks is the ampullae of Lorenzini, a system of special pores first described by Stephano Lorenzini in 1678. You can see these pores in the snouts of large sharks. They lead into the body and end in fluid or mucus-filled sacs.

For a long time, scientists believed that the ampullae helped sharks detect temperature or depth changes in the water. However, a recent number of experiments suggests that the ampullae actually may be used to sense very small changes in the electrical charge in the water. Shark researcher Dr. Arthur Myrberg of the University of Miami believes that sharks are more sensitive to electrical current than any other animal. Biological organisms give off different electrical charges and, at close range, the shark apparently is able to pick up these charges and use them to identify and locate prey.

Sharks can hear with their bodies, and for a long while scientists suspected that they could *taste* with them as well. Distributed all along the shark's body, burrowed under specially-adapted denticles, are sensory pit organs that structurally resemble tastebuds. These are sensitive to the state of the water, though exactly how they work or what they are for is not known.

Framed against a watery sky, a shark glides over a tropical reef in the Coral Sea near Australia.

Many beaches all over the world are protected by shark nets.
This net, at Kirra, Australia, has entangled two sharks.

An underwater cinematographer turns his movie camera lights on to film two "sleeping" sharks in an underwater cave off the Yucatan peninsula. Scientists have yet to explain why pelagic sharks retire to these caves.

"Dinner on a dolphin" for a blue shark.

A hooked whaler shark caught while eating turtle hatchlings.

Its unusual mouth with curved dental plates gives the horn shark a rather piglike appearance when viewed from the front. Its "horn" is a spine that protrudes at the front edge of the dorsal fins. Horn sharks are rarely longer than five feet.

A great white shark attacks an underwater photographer in a shark cage off the coast of Australia.

Remarkably camouflaged with marble coloring and "tasseled" skin around its head, a five-foot wobbegong shark rests under a ledge on Australia's Great Barrier Reef.

A grey nurse shark patrols nighttime waters off Australia.

Still, it's eerie. Here are all these denticles on the shark's skin, together with organs resembling taste-buds. It's as though the whole shark were just one huge mouth — as though the mouth between its frightening jaws weren't quite enough.

If a shark's hearing is impressive, his sense of smell is no less so. He has been described as a "swimming nose." He can detect scent in the water — and possibly *on* the water — up to hundreds of yards away. Experiments in Hawaii have demonstrated the shark's particular sensitivity to blood in the water. It was proven that he can detect one part of human blood in 100 million parts of water. Fully two-thirds of the seven-inch brain in an eight-foot shark is devoted to the smelling function.

The shark's sense of sight, on the other hand, still is a matter of debate. Some scientists feel that it is not as well developed as the other senses; others believe that it is comparable to man's. The shark

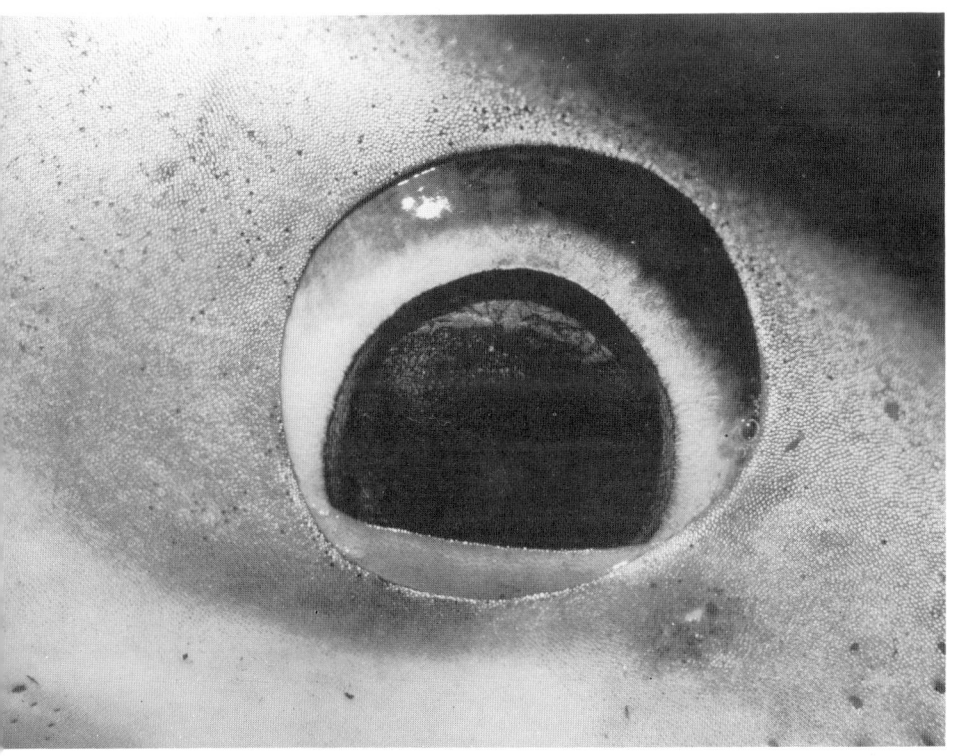

A shark's eye, with the nictitating membrane clearly visible.

may have trouble with color and with details, but he can accurately distinguish moving forms, and probably can see very well in dim light. A layer of cells behind each of his eyes, called the tapetum lucidum, reflect back to the eye images perceived in very dim light. In effect, the shark gets a chance to see everything twice in dim light. When he is in bright light, the tapetum lucidum is covered by another structure.

In addition to eyelids that only partially close, most sharks have a nictitating membrane — a very tough, second lower lid that can close over the entire eye. It is believed that the membrane protects the eye from physical or chemical irritants in the water.

When all of his senses lock onto prey, nothing can stop the shark. He becomes almost insane when attacking, particularly if he is feeding with a number of others. He seems to go mad when his sense of smell is stimulated by blood in the water, or his sense of hearing picks up the sound of another shark biting through bone. The result is what Dr. Gilbert, one of the world's foremost authorities on sharks, has called the "feeding frenzy." During this frenzy, nothing in the water is safe — not even the feeding sharks themselves. They may be attacked and eaten by their fellows.

Feeding sharks have been known to sustain horrible wounds, and go right on feeding. There is a story — not very pretty, but believed by most scientists and shark fishermen. It was first related in *Field Book of Giant Fishes*, published in 1949. This particular shark was caught by fishermen. It was hauled up to the deck of the boat, slit open, and gutted. After lying in the open air for a time, it was thrown back into the sea — presumably dead. But almost immediately it was caught again, this time on a hook baited with its own entrails.

A Varied Diet

For many centuries, sharks were considered scavengers, feeding off whatever dead meat came their way. They were thought to be cowardly, stupid, and completely indiscriminating in what they ate. Many sharks *are* indiscriminating, but they certainly are not cowards who will always await the easy meal.

It is true that sharks often followed sailing vessels, feeding off the garbage thrown overboard. They were very capable of keeping up with these small, slow ships. The casual swimming rate of mature sharks is about two and a half feet per second, and in controlled tests they have swum over 40 miles per hour in short bursts.

They were a constant escort to the slave ships of the 17th and 18th centuries. They followed the ships in large packs, and often were rewarded with the bodies of slaves who had died from the horrible conditions in the packed holds of the galleys.

Fishermen who have caught sharks and cut open their stomachs have found the widest assortment of "food" that can be imagined. In their book *The Natural History of Sharks,* Lineaweaver and Backus report that the stomach of one shark caught in Australia contained a goat, a turtle, a large tomcat, three birds, four fish heads, numerous other fish, and another shark six feet long.

Among the other treasures that have been found in their stomachs are grass, tin cans, a cow's head, 47 buttons, 25 one-quart bottles of water, a nearly whole reindeer, paper cups, a yellow-billed cuckoo, and a headless man in full armor. One can only guess how sharks came by some of these objects, but it becomes clear why they need the ability to get rid of indigestibles by everting their stomachs.

Sharks will eat almost anything, including each other. Some species, like the bull shark, actually seem to *prefer* shark meat, though they rarely will eat members of their own species. Most sharks will attack almost anything, too. The mako shark *(Isurus oxyrinchus),* which grows to 12 feet and weighs about 1,000 pounds, is one of the most beautiful of sharks and a favorite of sport fisherman. He is fond of attacking boats. Many fishermen have reported

Dr. Perry Gilbert examines a mako shark at close quarters.

mako attacks. It may be the smell of fish residue that attracts them, since in most cases where men were knocked overboard, the mako did not attack them. Many sharks lock onto a particular prey, and seem unaware of the presence of other food that does not fulfill the sensory signals to which they were first drawn.

4

The World of Sharks

Queequeg no care what god made him shark . . . wedder Fejee god or Nantucket god, but de god wat made shark must be one dam Ingin.

Herman Melville, Moby Dick, 1851

Man-eater

Of the 300 or so species of shark, about 25 will attack man. But the great white is the only species that everyone agrees will not only attack man but will eat him as well.

The great white shark is variously known as white death, man-eater, white shark, white pointer, and blue pointer. His scientific name is *Carcharodon carcharias.*

The great white looks the part of a killer. His body is fusiform, broad in the middle and tapered at both ends, rather like a torpedo. The form is hydrodynamic — adapted for efficient movement through water. The white shark's snout comes almost to a point. His tail, or caudal fin, is shaped like a crescent moon; the upper lobe is almost the same size as the lower lobe. In other sharks, the upper lobe often is much larger than the lower. In one family, the Chlamydoselachidae, the lower lobe is barely visible at all; these sleek sharks look like giant eels.

The great white is equipped with an impressive array of fins that help stabilize him in the water. On his sides are the large pectoral, or chest fins. On his back are two dorsal fins — a large front fin that protrudes from the water when he is swimming on the surface, and a smaller fin located well back toward the tail. Unlike the fins of other fish, these are not collapsible. They remain forever upright and firm as the shark glides through the water. Just behind and below the pectoral fins are the paired pelvic fins, and farther back is a single anal fin. Some sharks have only one dorsal fin; some have pelvic fins but no anal fin. Our great white, however, has them all.

The white shark is not white. He may be a variety of dirty shades of gray or blue or brown on the top and sides, and a dirty off-white underneath. There are dark smudges on his body where the pectoral fins are attached. These smudges look a little like "hair" under his "arms."

The great white shark is a deep sea, or pelagic, species, generally if not always a loner. It is a mystery why this deep sea fish appears inshore and near beaches as often as he does. Some experts believe that sharks who move in toward shore may be old and no longer able to compete for food in the deep seas. Others think they may be rogues — sharks who have tasted human flesh and have developed a liking for it.

Whatever the reason, great whites have been responsible for more unprovoked attacks on man than members of any other species. The great white probably is the most frightening creature alive today — with the single exception of man himself.

The great white shark is a direct descendant of one of the greatest sea monsters of all time — a shark that grew 60 to 80 feet long and weighed 100,000 pounds. The scientific name for this beast, *Carcharodon megalodon,* means "rough-toothed, huge-toothed." Indeed, it had teeth that were four inches wide at the base.

A battered monarch of the sea — a great white shark — whose scars show everything didn't always go his way in life.

Most scientists believe that *Carcharodon megalodon* has been extinct for at least 10,000 years, and perhaps much longer. But others believe that he still may be with us — that, in fact, he may be just an oversized great white. James F. Clark of the Museum of Comparative Zoology at Harvard sees no reason to suppose that these giants must necessarily be extinct. They would naturally be deep sea fish, rarely seen on the surface, probably feeding on giant squid and other large fish of the pelagic seas. Because, like all sharks, they would have no swim bladders, they would sink after death to the unknown depths of the sea. If the whale population still can sustain itself on the available food supply in the ocean, why not *Carcharodon megalodon*?

In any event, all great white sharks sighted or caught by fishermen have been considerably smaller than *Carcharodon megalodon* is known to have grown. Still, the great white shark is the third largest species now living, and the largest with functional teeth. Those teeth, largest toward the front of the mouth, are triangular, serrated like a bread knife, and *sharp*. The shark chomps down on his prey with these teeth, then thrashes furiously with his head until a large chunk is torn from his victim. He swallows the chunk whole. The teeth are not adapted for chewing.

Great white sharks can grow about 25 feet long, though 40-foot white sharks have reportedly been sighted. The largest one ever taken was hauled up off Cuba in the 1940s. It measured 21 feet and weighed 7,302 pounds. The liver accounted for a full 1,000 pounds of the weight.

The record for the largest great white shark — indeed, the largest fish — ever taken on a rod and reel goes to Alf Dean of Victoria, Australia. In 1959, Dean caught a 16-foot 10-inch white shark that weighed 2,664 pounds.

Tiger of the Seas

All sharks have been called tigers of the sea, but there is only one true tiger shark — *Galeocerdo cuvieri*. It is the second most dangerous species of shark, responsible for some of the most vicious attacks on man.

The tiger shark gets its name from the vertical brown bars on its sides. The bars are very apparent in young sharks, then fade as the sharks grow and may disappear altogether in a fully mature adult. Fully mature, in this case, may mean 18 feet long and weighing over a ton. The teeth in a tiger shark would resemble those of the great white — triangular and serrated—except for the pronounced notch on one side that makes them look like small claws. The tiger's tail has a large upper lobe and a smaller lower lobe.

This giant doesn't seem to be picky about his diet. Stewart Springer, an avid shark fisherman as well as a scientist, has reported finding a two-pound coil of

Menacing jagged teeth make the sand tiger shark look quite dangerous. It is.

copper wire, an unopened can of salmon, a good leather wallet, garbage, and assorted other artifacts in the stomachs of tiger sharks — in addition to the large fish that make up the main part of their diet. The snout of the tiger is shorter, blunter, and more rounded than the snout of the great white — still, as he approaches his prey in the water, he must be a terrifying creature indeed.

And he is fearless as well. In 1958, 8½-year-old Douglas Lawton was wading in three feet of water barely ten feet from shore. With him was his 12-year-old brother. They were in the waters of the Gulf of Mexico on the western coast of Florida. A tiger shark, later estimated to be only about five feet long, struck at Douglas' left leg. His brother came to his aid and managed to keep Douglas close to shore while other swimmers ran to help. Douglas' father grabbed the shark by the tail and pulled until it finally let go and swam away. However, the damage to Douglas' leg was so severe it had to be amputated above the knee.

A Modern Sea Monster

When scientists speak of "nature's mysteries," they're generally saying that nature knows just what it's doing, but science doesn't. High on the list of those mysteries is *Sphyrna zygaena* and his relatives in the Family Sphyrnidae: the hammerhead shark.

From the tip of its tail to just in front of its pectoral fins, the hammerhead could well be mistaken for any number of other sharks. But its head is the head of a sea monster. Rather than coming to a conical point, the head of this shark has projections on each side that make it resemble the crossbar of the letter *T*. The eyes are at the tips of the projections and command a very wide view of the surrounding sea.

Hammerheads are found the world over, and comprise several of the species that show a preference for their own kind in their diet. Shark fisherman Russell J. Coles once caught several hammerheads in his net (this species travels in groups, often very large groups). The largest of the hammerheads, a 14-foot monster, ate four of the others in the net, "two of which," wrote Coles, "she had just eaten whole, except the head of five-foot examples, and there were four cleanly-cut pieces which represented entire bodies, except the heads, of two more six-foot hammerhead sharks; then the stomach contained more than a peck of vertebrae of sharks." The hammerhead is also a menace to man, and has been blamed for many attacks around the world.

A favorite delicacy of hammerheads is sting rays. The venom of some rays is fatal to other fish and to man, but it doesn't seem to affect the hammerheads. Lineaweaver and Backus report that 54 sting ray spines were found in the throat, mouth, and jaws of one hammerhead that had been harpooned.

Bronco-busting with a speared hammerhead shark. Note the eye on the right side of the elongated head. This riddle of nature is a considerable threat to people.

Some of the spines were very fresh; nevertheless, the shark put up a huge fight when harpooned.

Shark expert Stewart Springer feels that the curious head may have evolved to aid the hammerhead in locating rays. Rays tend to burrow in the sand on the ocean floor. A hammerhead on the hunt might swim along the floor until his ampullae of Lorenzini detected the electrical current coming from a hidden ray; he could then unearth it by using his head as a sort of shovel.

Shark liver contains large amounts of Vitamin A, and the hammerhead's liver is particularly rich in this vitamin. For years, hammerheads were hunted for their livers, from which the vitamin was extracted. Vitamin A eventually was synthesized, and today, hammerheads are left pretty much alone by fishermen.

The Fox

Fishermen and sailors tell the story of a strange cooperation between the swordfish and the thresher shark. The thresher shark has a very long tail, sometimes accounting for half of his total length (which may reach 20 feet). The swordfish has a pointed, serrated snout that can pierce prey.

When the friends encounter a whale, the story goes, the thresher bangs on the prey's head and back with his tail. This drives the whale down to the waiting swordfish, who stabs the whale until it either drowns (whales must surface to breathe) or dies from the wounds. The whale is then eaten by the two predators.

The fact that neither the thresher nor the swordfish is physically capable of feeding on whales doesn't make any difference to the storytellers.

Be that as it may, the thresher *does* use his tail to get food. He has been observed in the midst of schools of smaller fish, thrashing about, gathering the fish into convenient clumps, which he then eats. In a dazzling display of coordination, he also can use the tail to flick a single fish into his mouth.

Many of the thresher's popular names have been inspired by his tail. Lineaweaver and Backus mention a few: thresher, thrasher, fox, sea-fox, swingle-tail, sea-ape, swiveltail, long-tailed shark, rat fish, mouse fish, and peacock shark. The thresher's scientific name is *Alopius vulpinus*. The first name is Greek and the second is Latin — and both mean "fox." Obviously, scientists have been impressed by that magnificent tail for a long time.

As a welcome change, the thresher shark never has been absolutely identified in an unprovoked attack on people. In a fish such as this, the tail would surely be as deadly as the jaws.

Sleepyhead

Sharks are found all over the world. Many species prefer warmer waters, and some even migrate seasonally to escape the cold. But there is at least one species, the Greenland shark, which prefers the frigid arctic zone.

The Eskimos, a hardy people known to eat practically anything, won't eat Greenland sharks except in emergencies. Unless carefully treated, the flesh is mildly poisonous, causing nausea and symptoms of drunkenness. The Greenland shark also is called the sleeper shark, because it moves slowly and seems very apathetic. When these sharks have been captured and cut open, however, their stomachs have contained such lively prey as squid, seals, and salmon. The shark's apparent lethargy may be caused by his need to conserve energy in the cold, demanding environment. But when he is feeding, he apparently can arouse enough fury to get a good meal.

The Greenland shark gives off the scent of ammonia, and the Eskimos have a legend to explain this. All other Greenland fish, the story goes, were created from wood, but not the shark. An old Eskimo woman was washing her hair in urine one day, as was the custom, and dried it with an old rag. A sudden gust of wind blew the rag out to sea, where it was transformed into *Somniosus microcephalus* — the Greenland shark.

Fresh Water Fiends

In 1526, Spanish historian Oviedo y Valdez wrote of the newly-discovered land of Nicaragua in Central America. He described its huge lake, and the marine life it contained.

Now, marine life is salt water life, and Lake Nicaragua is a fresh water lake.

There are sharks in Lake Nicaragua.

Over the centuries since Oviedo, scientists have pondered the question of fresh water sharks. Sharks have been discovered in lakes and rivers all over the world, but Lake Nicaragua, the largest fresh water body in Central America, has received the most attention. The lake empties into the Río San Juan, which flows 100 miles down to the Caribbean Sea. Fifteen miles north of Lake Nicaragua is Lake Managua. Though the two are connected by the Río Típitapa, there are no sharks in Lake Managua.

Scientists have long been puzzled by the travel habits of these sharks. No one knows if the sharks in Lake Nicaragua have always been there, or if they travel freely up and down the Río San Juan between the lake and the Caribbean.

In the early 1960s, Thomas B. Thorson of the University of Nebraska set out to answer this question. He doubted that the sharks were trapped in the lake, though many scientists had claimed that they must be; that somehow they must have found their way into fresh water and adapted to this very different medium. Other scientists felt that Lake Nicaragua had once been part of the Pacific Ocean, or the Caribbean Sea, and that changes in the earth's structure had turned it into a lake, trapping the marine life that was there.

Thorson found sharks all along the Río San Juan, even in the rapids. He captured specimens from many different areas of the lake and river, and found that they all came from the same species — *Carcharhinus leucas,* popularly known as the bull shark. He concluded that "there is no real basis for the belief that the shark population in the lake is landlocked," though he still had not proven that the sharks actually traveled from lake to sea.

Thorson then started a program of tagging sharks, a painless process similar to the tagging of other migratory animals. The results of this experiment are not yet in. However, most scientists will not be surprised if they reveal that the bull shark travels freely from salt to fresh water.

The freshwater bull shark and friend — a pilot fish. This killer was captured in the Zambesi River in Africa.

Then the problem will be to discover how they do it. The complex balance of water and salt in the bodies of fish should make it impossible for a shark to migrate from salt to fresh water and back again. However, we are all but certain the bull shark can do it.

Sharks are found in dozens of fresh water sites around the world, and everywhere they are considered very dangerous to man. In the United States, bull sharks have been found in the Atchafalaya River in Louisiana and the Pascagoula River in Mississippi. Sharks are not found in fresh water streams in the northern part of the country, but some species will venture up tidal streams where the water is salty or at least brackish. The attack on Charles VanZant was followed a few days later by a vicious multiple attack in Matawan, New Jersey, in a tidal stream several miles from the ocean.

Other fresh water rivers that have been plagued by shark attack are the Ganges in India and the Zambesi in southeast Africa. The sharks in both rivers have been almost positively identified as *Carcharhinus leucas* — the familiar bull shark of Lake Nicaragua.

The riddle of the fresh water bull shark is far from solved. If they are migratory, why don't they travel the last few miles above Lake Nicaragua and enter Lake Managua? Are the sightings of sharks *2,300 miles* up the Amazon in Peru legitimate? Why don't bull sharks enter fresh water rivers and lakes farther north than they now do? And how do their bodies adapt to the change in environment — an adaptation no other animal is able to make? Along with the question of how the hammerhead got that way, and hundreds of other questions about sharks, remains the mystery of the fresh water bull shark.

A Shark by Any Other Name . . .

Spiny dogfish is the popular name given to sharks of the Family Squalidae. Most of these sharks are small, seldom exceeding six to eight feet in length. But don't be fooled — they're still sharks. Many of them are as dangerous as the larger species, and some are even bolder.

All sharks of the Family Squalidae have a spine attached to the front of their dorsal fin. This is the single feature that distinguishes the very different members of this family.

One species, the spur dog or piked dogfish (*Squalus acanthias*), has the longest gestation period of any vertebrate animal. The mother shark may carry her young for 20 to 24 months before they are born.

Squalus acanthias only grows to three or four feet in length, and weighs only about ten pounds. But he can be a menace. The spines on his dorsal fins are sharp and mildly poisonous. He can lash out with them at anything that makes him angry. In the United States, he is considered a pest because he often destroys fishing equipment. But in Great Britain he is fished commercially and makes up part of the country's favorite light meal—fish and chips.

Another member of the Family Squalidae is the Portuguese shark *(Centroscymnus coelolepis)*. Portugal fished this shark commercially for a time. It is found in the Mediterranean and on both sides of the Atlantic. The Portuguese shark prefers extremely deep water — one was brought up from the record depth of 8,922 feet, over a mile and a half beneath the surface of the ocean. The Portuguese shark has huge eyes — the better to see anything at all in those depths.

Isistius brasiliensis of the Squalidae family is bioluminescent — it creates its own light. Some other dogfish also can create light, but none does it as well as *Isistius brasiliensis*. The mystery is not *how* the light is made. We know that some animals have light-producing organs called photophores.

The mystery is why. Members of this species have small fins, which suggests that they don't do much swimming. Perhaps they rely upon their bioluminescence to attract prey in the dark. Or perhaps the light is used for defense purposes. Some scientists feel that it may have something to do with sexual recognition between males and females of the species. The actual explanation is not known.

Isistius brasiliensis is less than two feet long at maturity, but is a vicious fighter when hooked or netted. Like all sharks, it is to be feared and respected — and never provoked — in the water or out.

5
Friends and Enemies

You can't eat your friends and have them too.
                                                                    Budd Schulberg

A Shark's Best Friend

Sharks seem the most friendless creatures in existence. The white shark is a loner, rarely seen in groups of any size at all. Most species that do travel in groups carefully arrange themselves according to size. If they didn't, the large ones would all too quickly consume the small ones. Separation by sex is widespread among shark populations, probably for the same reason — the larger females can be a substantial threat to the males.

Sharks lead a solitary existence. Dr. Myrberg has observed the tendency of some sharks in a group to give way to others, indicating a simple social awareness similar to the "pecking order" in a yardful of chickens. He believes that the shark's social organization may be more developed than we suspect. As yet, however, scientists have found no well-developed group identity in large shark populations.

Though they are avoided by almost all other life forms and hated by many, sharks do have companions, and strange little ones they are.

The pilot fish is a bony fish with vertical stripes around its body and several free-standing spines in front of its dorsal fin. It is often found in the company of large sharks. For a long time, people believed that the pilot fish acted as a guide (or pilot) for the sharks, leading its huge companions to their favorite foods and being rewarded with the scraps. The idea that sharks need guides is nonsense, but for many years it seemed the most logical explanation for the pilot fish's ability to get along in peace with the much larger, carnivorous sharks.

It is now believed that the pilot fish survive either because they are too quick for the sharks, or because they simply aren't very tasty to the particular sharks they accompany. The second explanation seems a little weak, since sharks will eat practically anything that moves—and much that doesn't. Pilot fish often follow other large fish, too, and

Slender, with a sharp, pointed nose, the blue shark is fairly common throughout the world's oceans in both tropical and temperate waters. Here, a blue shark is accompanied by a pilot fish.

A large nurse shark lies on the bottom of a tropical reef. A remora hovers above.

even have been seen burrowing within the tentacles of various jellyfish. However, they rarely follow great white sharks — possibly because this species is so fast and so vicious.

Another shark companion is the remora. Unlike the pilot fish, the remora doesn't just tag along — he actually attaches himself to the shark by means of a sucking disc on top of his head. Remoras aren't particular about the company they keep. They will attach themselves to whales, swordfish, turtles, hulls of ships, and glass aquariums, as well as to sharks. Paul Budker, in The Life of Sharks, describes one remora's attempt to attach itself to an underwater fisherman in West Africa. The fisherman had to flee, striking out at the remora as it followed him right up to the shore.

The remora's hold on his "host" can be tremendous. Tests have shown that an average-sized remora can grip with the strength of 100 pounds or more. Once a remora is attached, there is only one easy way to remove him — push him forward against the object of his attachment. If you pull him back, you probably will rip the disc from his body before you get him to let go.

Men have known about the remora since the time of Aristotle (fourth century B.C.). Back then, people believed that remoras could halt ships by attaching themselves to the hulls and exerting their natural forces. Such nonsense was the product of two separate but coincidental facts: the remora's tendency to attach itself to the hulls of ships, and the strange phenomenon known as "dead water."

Dead water occurs in coastal regions where a layer of fresh or brackish water lies on top of a mass of salt water. When a slow sailing vessel passes through, it sets up a pattern of waves. As the waves of the salt water rise high enough to reach the hull of the ship, the ship may slow down or stop altogether. In centuries gone by, sailors who dived to investigate the problem often found remoras attached to the hull, and so a legend was born. It had a long life. V. W. Ekman, a Swedish scientist, finally discovered the secret of dead water in 1906.

His Own Worst Enemy

It has been said that the shark is like man in that neither has any natural enemy except himself. This, of course, is not quite true. There are many organisms capable of preying on man, ranging from parasitic bacteria to large, wild animals.

Sharks may be the most terrifying creatures in the sea, but they, too, *do* have enemies. Sharks have been found in the stomachs, not only of other sharks, but of killer whales.

There are few animals that hunt and kill the shark for food, but many can defend themselves adequately against an attack. Dolphins have been known to gang up on an attacking shark. Dolphins are mammals, quite intelligent, and even more powerful swimmers than sharks. With their pointed snouts, they rush up underneath the shark and strike, disturbing the shark's swimming rhythm and possibly even damaging its internal organs. A shark hassled like this will eventually flee. Giant squid, crocodiles, and alligators can attack sharks and tear them apart.

There is a fish called the porcupine fish which, when gulped by a shark, can inflate its body, lodge itself in the shark's mouth, and prevent the shark from passing water through its gill slits and breathing. Once the shark is dead, the porcupine fish deflates and happily wanders out to freedom again — provided, of course, the shark died with its mouth open.

But, as with man, the shark remains his own *worst* enemy. Nature must strike a balance among all her millions of living things, and cannibalism among sharks is a vital factor in limiting their numbers. Natural enemies of the shark are not finally capable of the role when confronted with the shark's incomparable savagery.

6

The Shark in Legend

That I may win praise this day
I shall rescue the dear one this day
This is thy charm Lord Awao
This is thy charm Awao-throwing-gall-on-sharks.

Religious chant to protect a man in a canoe, W. G. Ivens, Mellanesians of the S. E. Solomon Islands, 1927

Shark legends are found throughout the world, though they are most varied in the South Pacific. In his book, *The Shark,* Philippe Cousteau discusses the legend of Kama-Hoa-Lii, the shark king of the Hawaiian Islands. He ruled the other sharks from his cavern outside the waters of Honolulu. He was a god, divine and immortal. But more than that — Kama-Hoa-Lii was *good.* He was believed to protect swimmers and guide home lost fishing vessels. To the Hawaiians and other island peoples, the shark was a being to be respected — feared perhaps, but never hated. Indeed, sharks often were worshiped as benefactors of mankind.

It is difficult to believe that the Hawaiians were not occasionally attacked and killed by sharks. They were. It also is difficult to believe a shark ever guided a lost boat home. The shark's habit of circling prey and often not attacking at all may account for the Hawaiians' belief that they were being protected from more dangerous fish — if there are any.

In any event, Kama-Hoa-Lii was a friend to man. He could assume a man's shape — an ability shared by gods of many different cultures. As a man, Kama-Hoa-Lii occasionally fathered human children, and if they were males, these children took on the powers of their father. Their backs were said to have the jaw-like marking of a shark, and their human guardians were warned to keep them away from meat. The Hawaiians were aware of the cannibalistic instincts of sharks — if Sonny got hold of roast pig one night, Mom and Dad might be dinner the next.

The Hawaiians believed in reincarnation — returning to life after death in some other body, often that of an animal. The very wise men of Hawaii were expected to be reincarnated as sharks. These men were granted special privileges while alive, and it is believed that their bodies were consigned to the deep after death—so their souls would be restored to the living body of the shark. Children who were born dead were wrapped in fruits and sacred roots and also buried at sea, in hopes that the gods there would accept the souls.

Attitudes toward sharks differed greatly from culture to culture in Polynesia. On some islands, the shark had much the same reputation as he had in Hawaii. On others, he was just a big fish that attacked and ate people every now and then.

On a number of islands, sharks (and often other fish, birds, and animals) were believed to be reincarnations of ancestors, and therefore sacred. Families tried to tame these creatures, and on no account were they harmed. You might cook somebody else's grandfather for lunch, but it was a religious crime to destroy an animal sacred to your own family.

Some island parents intentionally brought their children together with sharks to teach them to deal calmly with this constant threat. The practice undoubtedly produced mixed results.

The more "sophisticated" civilizations of the western world were not without their legends and superstitions about sharks. In Europe during the 16th century, sailors believed it was bad luck to come across a hammerhead shark. If a female hammerhead was caught, it was a warning of fearful things to come. The tail of a porpoise or shark traditionally was nailed to the ship as protection against the forces of the sea, and sailors might refuse to board their vessels until this was done.

Shark parts — teeth, jaws, fins, and internal organs — were credited with magical powers. In Europe, the teeth were set in gold, and supposedly protected children from evil in the night and gave them good appetites. Shark teeth also were used to detect poison in food. They were supposed to change color when placed in food that had been poisoned. Some people believed that they destroyed the powers of poison in food. Getting rid of one's enemies by poisoning them passed out of general fashion after the sixteenth century — and so, apparently, did the belief in the magical powers of shark teeth.

Early pharmacists treated such ailments as gall-stones, cataracts, ringworm, and bad teeth with a variety of concoctions made from shark organs, mainly the brain and liver. Though the liver *is* rich in Vitamin A, it is not certain just what value these early medicines had.

Though modern man no longer worships the shark as a god, he does seem to fear the shark as a sort of devil. Sharks often are the targets of hysterical hatred by otherwise gentle and civilized people. Beached sharks have been attacked by normally calm, sane individuals who hack at them with jack-knives, gouge their eyes, and cut away their jaws for spite — and for souvenirs. Our age-old fears and prehistoric savagery are still with us.

7
The Best Defense

The natural conclusion is that the shark offers no unusual hazards to a swimming or drifting man. . . .

U.S. Navy manual, Shark Sense,
1944 edition

Sashes to Shark Chaser

Different cultures have handled the threat of shark attack in different ways. In Japan, divers tied long red sashes around their waists to ward off sharks (perhaps some still do — superstition dies slowly). Ceylon had shark charmers. Before divers entered the water, the shark charmer performed a religious service designed to exorcise the evil power of the sharks, or drive them from the area altogether. Marco Polo first described the shark charmers in 1298; the post was handed down from father to son, and there still are shark charmers in Ceylon today.

In the United States, the threat of shark attack was minimized for many years. Right up until World War II, many Americans refused to believe that sharks were all that dangerous. It took some pretty nasty incidents to change their minds.

Paul Budker tells the story of Herman Oelrichs, who was so certain that sharks would not attack north of the waters of North Carolina that he offered a reward of $500 to anyone who could prove otherwise. This was in 1890, and when Oelrichs died in 1906, no claims had been made on his offer. Ten years later came the attack on Charles VanZant in New Jersey. That attack was followed a few days later by several other attacks, finally resulting in four people killed and one crippled. Two days after the last attacks, an eight-and-a-half-foot great white shark was netted near the area. In its stomach were 15 pounds of human flesh and bones, including the shinbone of a boy and a human rib.

In 1942, at the height of World War II, the British ship *Nova Scotia* was torpedoed and sunk by a German submarine. The *Nova Scotia* was on its way to South Africa, and on board were 765 Italian prisoners of war and 134 South African soldiers. Most of the lifeboats were destroyed in the attack, leaving hundreds of survivors swimming helplessly about.

Then the sharks came.

Some accounts say that the German submarine captain, realizing the horror of what he had done, surfaced his ship, radioed for help, and aided survivors. Other accounts make no mention of this dangerous sacrifice on the captain's part.

But over 800 of the almost 1,000 men on board perished, many in the jaws of sharks.

Not long afterward, the U.S. Navy issued its manual, *Shark Sense*. It repeated the prevailing view — that sharks posed no unusual threat — attempting to soothe the fears of Navy personnel and pilots.

But at the same time, the Navy began a search for an effective shark repellent. The crash program was headed by Stewart Springer, and involved a number of other scientists. Many different things — chlorine, poison gases, sound vibrations — were tested, but nothing worked. Sharks *could* be killed, but not quickly enough to prevent them from attacking.

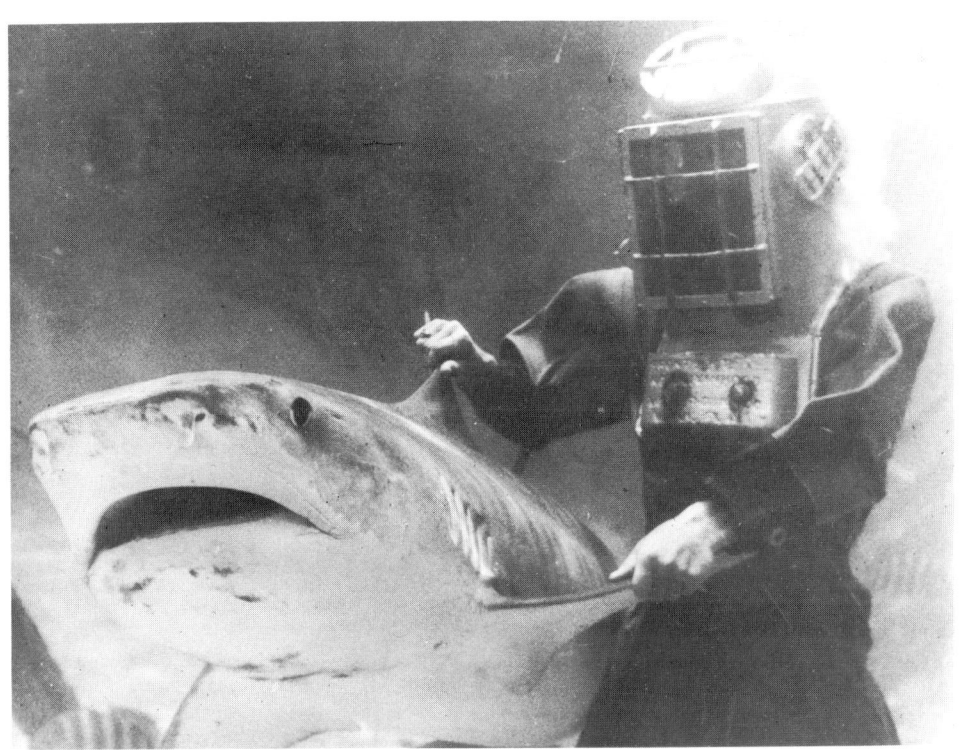

Walking the shark. This tiger was so exhausted by his struggles against captivity that water had to be forced over his gills in order to revive him.

The scientists finally came up with Shark Chaser, a 6½-ounce cake of black dye that contained copper acetate. The dye helped hide men in the water; the acetate, a substance produced by the decaying flesh of sharks, was believed to cause a reaction in sharks that resembled fear.

The men's spirits were lifted somewhat when Shark Chaser was distributed, but the fact that it boosted morale was its primary claim to fame. The problem was, and is, that it really doesn't work. When dealing with sharks, some methods work some of the time on some species. Others are a waste of time, or even worse, provoke attack.

In 1958, the Shark Research Panel was formed to search for a better shark repellent. The panel was headed by Dr. Perry Gilbert, and included 36 other scientists. Over the next 13 years, they tested 200

A diver approaches a dead shark, awesome even in death.

biological and chemical repellents, including nicotine, strychnine, and other poisons. Some were injected into different species; some were simply released in the water. The scientists finally had to admit defeat. Many of the chemicals they tested had no effect at all, while others, though eventually calming or killing the sharks, didn't take effect soon enough to be effective repellents.

The problem is that depressant drugs produce an excitation phase first. A chemical dispersed in the water around a swimmer must make its way to the shark's bloodstream and then to his brain, where its first effect will be to excite the fish. By the time the depressant effect takes hold, the swimmer might well be part of the shark's digestive system.

Dr. H. David Baldridge, a chemist and shark expert who has spent many years seeking an effective shark repellent, has said that the Shark Chaser packet issued to military personnel would have to be strengthened 50 to 100 times to begin to produce the desired effect.

Though we don't yet know what repels sharks, we do know some of the things that attract them. Seals are part of the natural diet of some sharks, and it is thought that a diver in a black wet suit often can be mistaken for a seal. Many divers now wear blue or green suits, and not only for the fashion value.

But color must be treated carefully. After World War II, it was discovered that the new, brilliant orange Navy life jackets tended to attract sharks Even if the sharks' color sense isn't good (and we're not sure of that), bright objects do attract them. So do sharp contrasts in color—for instance, a suntanned swimmer in a white suit.

Many divers, among them Jacques-Yves Cousteau, now carry "billy clubs" as a defense against sharks. These are heavy pieces of wood, shaped like a policeman's nightstick, attached to the diver's wrists by a leather or hemp thong. The club may be weighted in the end and studded with nails. A sharp rap on the snout with one of these often will drive away a shark.

The crew of filmmakers who went in search of the great white shark for the movie *Blue Water, White Death* used a more deadly version of the billy club, called a "bang stick." Their journey is recorded in Peter Matthiessen's book, *Blue Meridian*. The bang stick is a specially adapted billy club that actually explodes a shotgun charge against the shark.

Peter Gimbel, who headed the filmmaking expedition, has swum between the mouths of sharks while they were feeding on whales. This example of almost foolhardy courage is not to be followed by anyone. But Gimbel does have some good thoughts on how to handle an attacking shark. He is careful in his conclusions:

"The shark is not a mammal and it's a form of life

far removed from any mammal; it's an eating machine. Trickery won't work, or craftiness or cunning, as it wouldn't work against an insane mind. . . . When you come up against that quality of the passionless killer, you're in bad trouble."

Some people feel that it's terribly dangerous to use a billy club or a bang stick against a shark, but Gimbel disagrees. "This idea that you mustn't provoke them is nonsense," he says. "If you *really* hurt one, he'll go find something easier to eat." Of course, a bang stick won't prevent a shark from attacking; it only provides a defense if he does.

The most reliable shark *protection* now available is the Johnson shark screen, named for its inventor, Dr. C. Scott Johnson. The shark screen is a tall container resembling a plastic bucket. It is filled with salt water, and the person is suspended inside. Inflatable rings around the top keep the "bucket" afloat. The screen not only hides the person from the shark's vision (it is black, and does not reflect light well) — it also keeps the person's scent out of the water. Since sharks tend to stay away from objects larger than themselves, the screen is most effective with sharks less than eight feet long. However, it is of some use with larger species as well. The screen offers the greatest hope yet for victims of shipwreck and air disasters.

Though a chemical repellent has not been found, scientists have experienced some success with *physical* repellents. One is the parachute dart. A standard dart gun is equipped with a special dart that contains a small parachute. The parachute opens when the dart is imbedded in the shark's body. It impedes his swimming, and his mind is taken off prey while he tries to dislodge it. A similar weapon is the CO_2 cartridge, which discharges carbon dioxide gas into the shark's body and upsets his balance. The shark tends to lose all thought of eating, and experiences violent convulsions that may be fatal.

Shark armor is being tested, too. The armor is not meant to repel sharks, but to save the diver from injury if he is attacked. It will be a tall order to come up with an effective armor, however. Some sharks can bite with the pressure of 18 metric tons per square inch, enough to cut through practically anything.

The Navy manual, *Shark Sense,* has been revised and updated. Among the new material is a statement that should always be remembered, no matter how safe you feel in the water: "Never count on a shark not attacking you. He may do it."

Attack File

The Shark Research Panel, whose primary goal was to find an effective repellent, also set up a system to record shark attacks worldwide. Every effort was made to gather as much material as

A wrong turn landed this 30-foot, 10,000-pound whale shark on a beach in Australia. Its gaping mouth poses a threat to little besides sea plankton.

possible about every verifiable attack that had ever occurred. The International Shark Attack File contains reports on attacks from 1580 to the present, and offers a wealth of information, some of it quite surprising.

For one thing, only about three dozen people are attacked each year. The mortality rate is 35 percent overall, but has been falling recently — probably due to advances in transporting and caring for victims — until today's rate is about 16 percent. This means that only six people are actually killed by sharks every year. Small numbers indeed to cause such widespread fear of sharks.

All statistics must be read very carefully. For instance:

Two-thirds of all attacks take place in water no more than five feet deep.

Thirteen males are attacked for each female.

Among the 83 documented cases of attacks on submerged skin divers, *none* was female.

We cannot conclude from these statistics that most sharks are found in water no more than five feet deep. However, most *swimmers* are. The fact that men are attacked more often than women presents something of a problem. Most skin divers probably are male, though there certainly are not 13 men at beaches for every woman. Females in the water may have different swimming motions, less attractive to sharks. Or they may give off a different scent. No one really knows.

Dr. Baldridge has been in charge of the Shark Attack File since the late 1960s. His book, *Shark Attack,* thoroughly describes the findings in the file, and is one of the most grisly, though fascinating, scientific publications ever printed. Dr. Baldridge points out that perhaps as many as half to two-thirds of all shark attacks are not made for feeding purposes. In a typical attack, there are lacerations, but actual tissue loss is rare. Many attacks end after a single bite or slash. Sharks may attack for many reasons, but it seems clear that they are not particularly fond of human flesh in their diet. If they were, there would be thousands of attacks a year, instead of approximately three dozen, and the majority would be fatal.

Unfortunately, the International Shark Attack File has fallen into disuse — the victim of funding problems. Much that was learned from information in the file had a profound effect on shark research. Its absence is sorely felt by the scientific community, and it should be revitalized through government or private grants as soon as possible.

Don't Go Near the Water

In addition to its other work, the Shark Research Panel tackled the problem of protecting beaches

Underwater photographer Mary Roessler confronts a leopard shark on Australia's Great Barrier Reef.

from sharks. Hundreds of millions of people visit beaches every year, and it is here that most shark attacks occur.

Some divers reported that sharks fled from the bubbles emitted from their air tanks, so commercial interests in Atlantic City, New Jersey, decided to install bubble curtains outside the swim lines at their beaches. The panel was called upon to test the devices first. Dr. Gilbert's staff found a shark or two that would refuse to enter the experimental curtain they set up, but most species had a ball passing through the bubbles. Obviously, a bubble curtain was not going to work. Atlantic City saved about $100,000, and the panel, according to Dr. Gilbert, earned the undying hatred of a couple of air compressor companies.

Electric repellers were tested with uneven success. Enclosing beaches with steel mesh fences is effective but expensive; fences cannot be used at all in areas that have strong currents.

One method used with great success in Natal, South Africa, is enclosing beaches with net meshing — essentially a fishing operation. Until Natal installed the nets, its beaches had been plagued by shark attacks.

Led by shark expert Beulah Davis, the meshing operation has produced some of the safest beaches in the world. Only two attacks, neither of which was fatal, have occurred along the 200-mile coastline over the last ten years.

Thirty-nine of Natal's beaches are protected with 238 gill nets. A shark can get his head through a gill net, but his forward motion is eventually stopped by his pectoral fins. The net then gets stuck around his gills, and he is held fast. Most sharks cannot stop swimming for long, nor can they back up. When caught in a gill net, they suffocate. The nets are regularly hauled up, emptied of their catch, and replaced. They are set in overlapping rows, forming a simple maze that is a very effective trap.

Beaches in Natal can accommodate this type of protection. Others around the world cannot, though meshing is used widely in Australia as well. Dr. Gilbert has suggested one economical way of protecting beaches in the United States: encourage shark fishermen to fish these areas, thus controlling shark populations.

The odds against being attacked by a shark are phenomenally high. Most swimmers will never even see a shark, much less have to deal with one at close range. A person probably has a greater chance of being struck by lightning on three separate occasions than of being attacked by a shark even once; more people die of practically every other cause imaginable — including alcoholism, mosquito bites, climbing mountains, and playing in streets — than are killed by sharks.

Still, the very *possibility* is enough to send a chill down the spine. It doesn't hurt to be prepared — just in case.

Dr. Gilbert has proposed a number of guidelines for ocean bathers. Never swim alone. A companion may discourage a shark from attacking, or be an aid if he does. In many cases, rescuers who have come to the aid of an attack victim have not been attacked themselves. Many sharks seem to develop a sensory lock on a victim, and cannot easily break off a concentrated attack to deal with another threat. Two or more swimmers together may prevent him from developing the lock at all.

If dangerous sharks are known to be in the area, stay out of the water. This may seem obvious, but humanity is a strange breed, known to do foolish things for the adventure of it.

Don't enter or remain in the water if you have an open wound, even if it is only a scratch. Dangerous sharks may detect blood in the water from 200 yards away or more, depending on the movement of the current.

Don't swim in murky water where your visibility is poor. Remember, sharks do not rely on their vision to find you. Most shark attack victims never see what hit them.

If a shark is sighted, get out of the water quickly, but without panic. We know that dogs can detect fear; scientists are trying to determine if sharks can, too. They certainly are attracted to vigorous thrashing in the water.

If you are swimming in a group when a shark is sighted, get everyone to bunch up in a circle facing outward, and move to shore. The bulk alone may discourage a shark from attacking.

If someone is attacked, make every effort to stop the bleeding and get the victim to medical facilities as fast as possible. Most shark attack deaths are caused by shock and/or excessive bleeding.

A shark can be discouraged from following through an attack. Striking him sharply on the snout may do the trick — if his rough skin doesn't open a wound on your hand. Swimmers who actually have been seized by sharks have successfully driven them off by gouging the shark's eyes, nostrils, or gill slits.

8
Some Uses for Sharks

FROM THE JAWS OF DEATH
Genuine MAKO SHARK TOOTH PENDANT
A most unique and original gift idea at $19.95
or His & Hers sets at $37.50. . . .

Magazine advertisement, 1975

The uses man has found for sharks have not caught up with the supply, so unlike such natural resources as oil, bison, and whales, most species of shark are not in serious trouble.

When the shark is fished today, it is often for sport. Taxidermists report that sharks represent about one-fourth of all big fish now being professionally stuffed. A few species are marvelous game fish — most notably the mako shark, cousin of the great white, who fights like the devil when hooked and leaps from the water in splendid exhibitions of savage strength.

In the past, some people indulged in a far more dangerous sport. In Hawaii, a shark would be driven into an arena built in a lagoon. A native, armed only with a shark tooth attached to the end of a stick, would enter the water and do battle with the mighty emissary of Kama-Hoa-Lii.

Santo Domingo, in the West Indies, had professional shark fighters, much like the professional bullfighters of Spanish-speaking countries. They

A shark fight in the Dominican Republic — lively sport, though considering the size of the knife and the shark, probably no more dangerous than Monday Night Football.

fought for a set payment, and were armed only with knives. As terrifying as this may seem, we must remember that sharks, though brutal and incredibly strong, are no match for professionals. Man has the advantage, for though his body is weak, his mind is quick.

There are a few additional uses for sharks. Some shark flesh is edible and even tasty, and is marketed around the world in a variety of disguises — most people would rather not know they are eating shark meat. It is sold as grayfish in the United States. The Orientals aren't afraid to face the facts, and shark fin soup has long been a delicacy with them.

The hides of sharks are sometimes used for leather goods — most notably for shoes and boots. But the denticles must be removed, and the hides carefully treated. This is an involved and expensive process. The demand for shark skin articles is relatively small, though it shows signs of increasing. The hides — with denticles intact — can be used for sandpaper and for the handles of swords, but synthetic material has almost entirely replaced shark hide.

Sharks are captured by the thousands for experimental purposes. In most cases, they are used to discover more about sharks. As we unravel the mysteries of this creature, we may begin to tap some of his secrets for our benefit. Perhaps these secrets will have to do with behavior. Perhaps medical research will reveal startling immunities to disease — immunities that man can learn to share. There may be a message for man in the fact that sharks have remained virtually unchanged for over 300 million years.

9
A Personal Note

In November, 1975, while this book was being written, I traveled to Orlando, Florida, to attend a conference on sharks.

Representatives from every corner of sharkdom were there: scientists, fishermen, beach protectors, public relations people who were nervous about their tourist trade. Most of the people mentioned in this book were there.

The jaws of a bull shark were tacked up on a bulletin board. I could see the spare teeth lying along the inside. Men and women were wearing shark tooth jewelry. The polished white teeth, set in gold or silver, hung from ears, necks, and wrists.

These were people whose lives revolved around sharks, who had devoted decades to studying them or fishing for them or fighting them. As I talked with them, I began to see a different view of sharks, one not bred of ignorance and unreasoning fear, but of real knowledge and respect.

Their intimate contact with sharks had resulted in admiration tinged with a comfortable humor. One panel discussed the causes of shark attack. Stewart Springer said that while he didn't deny that sharks may attack for food occasionally, he thought perhaps they enter beaches to have a little fun—some sport at our expense, just as we have so much at theirs.

Here were people who admired the shark's perfect form. Sharks may be savage, as the title of this book says, but more importantly, they are survivors. They have survived earthquake and ice age. They have survived oceans that no longer exist. They have survived evolution and they have all but survived time itself.

If they will survive man, only time will tell — but time is on their side. Today, there are more sharks eaten by people than people eaten by sharks. But, as Dr. Baldridge told me, there also are more people eaten by *people* than are eaten by sharks.

Speaking of food. On the last day of the conference, we had a real treat. A shark fisherman had flown in some shark meat and turned it over to the hotel cook. He deep-fried some of the bite-sized pieces, and sauteed others in a butter and wine sauce. When we came out of our last meeting, there was the shark, served up in a buffet for us.

I didn't know if he was a white or a hammerhead or a bull. I didn't know if he'd been touring the Indian Ocean or the Pacific Ocean or the South China Sea, though he could have come from anywhere. I didn't know if he'd ever had a piece of man inside him, or if he was one of the majority of species as threatening to us as a baby kitten.

But I knew he could swim with the speed of a gazelle. I knew the uncharted depths of the ocean trembled at his approach. I knew his great-great-grandfathers swam beside the galleons of Columbus, Cleopatra's barge, and the outrigger canoes of a hundred generations of South Sea islanders. I knew all this as I stood in the waiting line, paper plate in hand and a reluctant look on my face.

He was delicious.

Works Cited in this Book

Baldridge, H. David. *Shark Attack*. New York: Berkley Publishing Corporation, 1975.

Budker, Paul. *The Life of Sharks*. New York: Columbia University Press, 1971.

Cousteau, Jacques-Yves, and Philippe Cousteau. *The Shark: Splendid Savage of the Sea*. New York: Doubleday & Company, Inc., 1970.

Lineaweaver, Thomas H., III, and Richard H. Backus. *The Natural History of Sharks*. Philadelphia: J. B. Lippincott Company, 1973.

Matthiessen, Peter. *Blue Meridian*. New York: Random House, 1971.